Find out more

Books

Bugs and Spiders (Amazing Life Cycles), George C. McGavin (TickTock Books, 2014)

Ocean (Life Cycles), Sean Callery (Kingfisher Books, 2012)

The Life Cycle of Mammals (Life Cycles), Susan H. Gray (Raintree, 2011)

Websites

**www.childrensuniversity.manchester.ac.uk/interactives/science/
  microorganisms/mushroomlifecycle**
Follow this interactive story to find out all about how mushrooms reproduce.

www.ngkids.co.uk/did-you-know/butterfly-life-cycle
Visit the National Geographic Kids website for fascinating facts about the butterfly's life cycle.

www.oum.ox.ac.uk/thezone/animals/life/produce.htm
Uncover the secrets of the human life cycle.

HISTORY OF BRITAIN – THE ROMAN CONQUEST OF BRITAIN
was produced for Heinemann Children's Reference
by Lionheart Books, London

First published in Great Britain by Heinemann
Children's Reference, an imprint of Heinemann
Educational Publishers, a division of Reed
Educational and Professional Publishing Limited,
Halley Court, Jordan Hill, Oxford OX2 8EJ

MADRID ATHENS
FLORENCE PRAGUE WARSAW
PORTSMOUTH NH CHICAGO SAO PAULO MEXICO
SINGAPORE TOKYO MELBOURNE AUCKLAND
IBADAN GABORONE JOHANNESBURG KAMPALA NAIROBI

Editors: Lionel Bender, Sue Reid
Designer: Ben White
Editorial Assistant: Madeleine Samuel
Picture Researcher: Jennie Karrach
Media Conversion: Peter MacDonald
Educational Consultant: Jane Shuter
Editorial Advisors: Andrew Farrow, Paul Shuter

Production Controller: David Lawrence
Editorial Director: David Riley

ISBN 0 600 58832 7 Hb   ISBN 0 600 58835 5 Pb

British Library Cataloguing-in-Publication Data.
A catalogue record for this book is available from
the British Library.

Printed in Italy

Acknowledgements

Picture credits Pages 4 (top):C .M. Dixon. 5 (centre): Mick Sharp.
5 (bottom): National Museum of Wales/44.32/75. 6 (top, bottom),
7: C. M. Dixon. 8 (top): Courtesy of the Trustees of the British
Museum/ PS261195. 8 (bottom): Museum of London -PH95/306.
9: C. M. Dixon. 10 (top): C. M. Dixon. 10 (bottom): Courtesy of the
Trustees of the British Museum/PS129007. 12 (left): Courtesy of the
Trustees of the British Museum/ PS294933.12 (right): English Heritage
Heritage/ Skyscan Balloon Photography. 13: English Heritage
Photographic Library. 14 (top): Courtesy of the Trustees of the British
Museum/ PS294932. 15 (top): Courtesy of the Trustees of the British
Museum/ PS284406. 15 (bottom): University of Cambridge/
Committee of Aerial Photography. 16 (top): C. M. Dixon. 16 (bottom):
Collections/ Robert Hallmann. 17: Courtesy of the Trustees of the
British Museum/PS292769. 18: Museum of London/BGH95. 19 (top):
Museum of London/BUC 87. 19 (bottom): Museum of London/IT245.
20 (top): C. M. Dixon. 20 (bottom): Museum of London/6090.89.PDN
81. 22 (top): English Heritage Photographic Library. 22 (bottom left):
Mick Sharp. 22 (bottom right): Museum of London/249-69.

All artwork by John James except maps by Hayward Art Group.

Cover: Artwork John James. Photographs: Roman soldiers with
barbarian captives (C. M. Dixon); Celtic plaque (National Museum of
Wales); Roman tombstone (Gloucester City Museums/C. M. Dixon).

Every effort has been made to contact copyright holders of any mate-
rial reproduced in this book. Any omissions or errors will be rectified
in subsequent printings if notice is given to the Publisher.

PLACES TO VISIT

Here are some Roman and Celtic sites you can visit. Town
museums all over Britain have examples of Roman or pre-
Roman pottery and coins.

Bath, Avon. Roman baths and other buildings, museum.

Bigbury, Kent. Iron Age hill-fort.

Bignor, Sussex. Parts of villa can be seen.

Caerleon, Wales. Roman legionary fortress, barracks,
amphitheatre and museum.

Caerwent, Wales. Walls, gates and defences can still be
seen.

Chedworth, Gloucestershire. Museum and excavated remains
of villa.

Chester, Cheshire. Museum and remains of Roman fortress,
defences and amphitheatre.

Chichester, West Sussex. City and Guildhall museums have
Roman-British pottery and coins.

Cirencester, Gloucestershire. Museum, sections of town wall,
remains of amphitheatre.

Colchester, Essex. Museum and remains of walls, gates and
pre-Roman defences.

Dorchester, Dorset. Museum, amphitheatre.

Dover, Kent. Lighthouse on clifftop within walls of medieval
castle.

Fishbourne, West Sussex. Remains of palace of Cogidubnus.

Hadrian's Wall, Cumbria, Tyne & Wear. Sections of wall and
forts such as Housesteads, Vindolanda, Carrawburgh.

Hod Hill, Dorset. Hill-fort with remains of Roman auxiliary fort
in north-west corner.

Lincoln, Lincolnshire. Museum, parts of gates and town walls;
also sections of Roman road north and south.

London. British Museum and Museum of London; remains of
Roman city wall.

Lullingstone, Kent. Museum, parts of Roman villa.

Maiden Castle, Dorset. Enormous hill-fort and mounds to
walk over.

Richborough, Kent. Remains of shore defences,
amphitheatre, monument, and later fort.

Silchester, Hampshire. Museum and amphitheatre; most of
the Roman town is now beneath farmland.

St Albans, Hertfordshire. Walls, remains of Roman
Verulamium, including theatre, and remains of Celtic
settlement.

York, North Yorkshire. Museum and remains of legionary
fortress, partly under medieval cathedral or Minster.

Introduction

In AD 43 hundreds of ships sailed across the Channel and landed on a beach in Kent. Out of the ships came thousands of tough, heavily armed soldiers. It was the biggest invasion army yet to attack Britain – the beginning of the Roman conquest. Many Britons fought fiercely against the invaders. Others were ready to welcome them. For more than 40 years the Romans fought to seize control of southern Britain from its tribal chieftains. The Romans were backed by a mighty empire. Their eventual conquest made southern Britain part of the Roman world.

Contents

HOW ROME SAW BRITAIN

Before the Roman general Julius Caesar landed on its shores in 55 and again in 54 BC, few Romans knew much of Britain. The people of the island were Celts, living outside the Roman empire. But they knew of Rome and its power.

In the first century BC, much of Europe was governed by Rome. From the white cliffs of Dover, a British Celt could gaze across the Channel to Gaul (modern France). Gaul was a Roman province, won by conquest. British chieftains had sent warriors to Gaul to help their fellow Celts fight the Romans. Later, refugees from Gaul fled to Britain to escape Roman rule. From these events, the Romans learnt more about Britain. Traders also crossed the Channel from Gaul to buy the cloth and large hunting dogs for which the island was famous.

▷ **A Celtic shield.** Celtic warriors carried shields like this into battle. However, this shield was probably only used at ceremonies.

▽ **Trade between south-east Britain and Gaul.** The people in both lands were Celts, who lived in tribal groups, each with their own territory. Boulogne was the main port in Gaul for the cross-Channel trade.

Colchester
London
Canterbury
Medway
Dover • Richborough
• Calais
• Boulogne
GAUL
THE CHANNEL

Britain was split into many small tribal areas, each ruled by a chieftain. The people were farmers, living in villages and often fighting against one another. To defend themselves, they built hill-forts, with massive earth banks and intricately planned gateways. Warrior-nobles and Druid-priests ruled British Celtic society. Prisoners of war were sold as slaves.

Much of Britain was covered by thick forest, though large areas of woodland had been cleared for farming. There were no real roads, only trackways along which chieftains rode on horses, followed on foot by their servants. The ancestors of these Celtic warriors had arrived in Britain hundreds of years before. Now they were the rulers of the island, at home in a climate which the Roman historian Tacitus described as "objectionable, with frequent rains and mists".

◁ **A Celtic camp near Dover.** The houses had timber frames, with walls made from woven sticks and mud. A fence surrounded the settlement. Horses were used for riding and for pulling chariots, which the Celts often used in warfare. Dogs were also valued highly, especially for hunting deer and boar.

▽ **The Celts in Britain** usually fortified their villages against attack. This is a reconstruction of an Iron Age settlement at Castell Henllys, Newport, in Dyfed. The design of the round houses is based on archaeological evidence.

◁ **A silver plaque** found at Llyn Cerrig Bach in Anglesey, north Wales. This plaque was either worn as an ornament, or fastened to a chieftain's chariot. Luxury goods like this were made in Britain long before the Romans invaded the island. The Celts liked designs with coils and swirls, like leaves, and were famous for their skill in metalwork. British styles were influenced by trade with mainland Europe, including Gaul.

THE FIRST INVASION

Julius Caesar had conquered Gaul, where he had seen British Celts fighting with Gauls. His invasion of Britain was partly to punish them for this. Caesar was proud of his invasion troops: "The soldiers worked splendidly," he wrote.

▷ **A Roman ship carrying soldiers.** This is one of many scenes from a decorated column, built in Rome to celebrate the victories of the Emperor Trajan. The invasion ships had oars, so that they could be rowed up to the beach.

▽ **A Celtic dagger and sheath**, found in the River Thames, near Cookham in Berkshire.

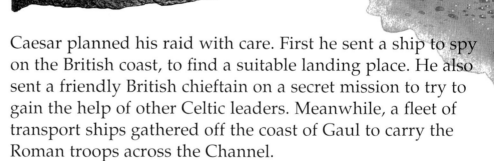

Caesar planned his raid with care. First he sent a ship to spy on the British coast, to find a suitable landing place. He also sent a friendly British chieftain on a secret mission to try to gain the help of other Celtic leaders. Meanwhile, a fleet of transport ships gathered off the coast of Gaul to carry the Roman troops across the Channel.

Caesar's spies reported a possible landing place near Dover. In the autumn of 55 BC, 80 Roman ships put to sea. The people of Kent had no warships to fight a fleet at sea. So the Romans were able to cross the Channel unopposed, and they landed on a beach not at Dover but at nearby Walmer. The landing was only partly successful. The Roman cavalry never reached the shore because its ships were driven off by storms. Without horsemen to fight the waiting Celts with their chariots, Caesar felt unsure of victory. After a few skirmishes with the enemy, he went back to Gaul to plan a second raid.

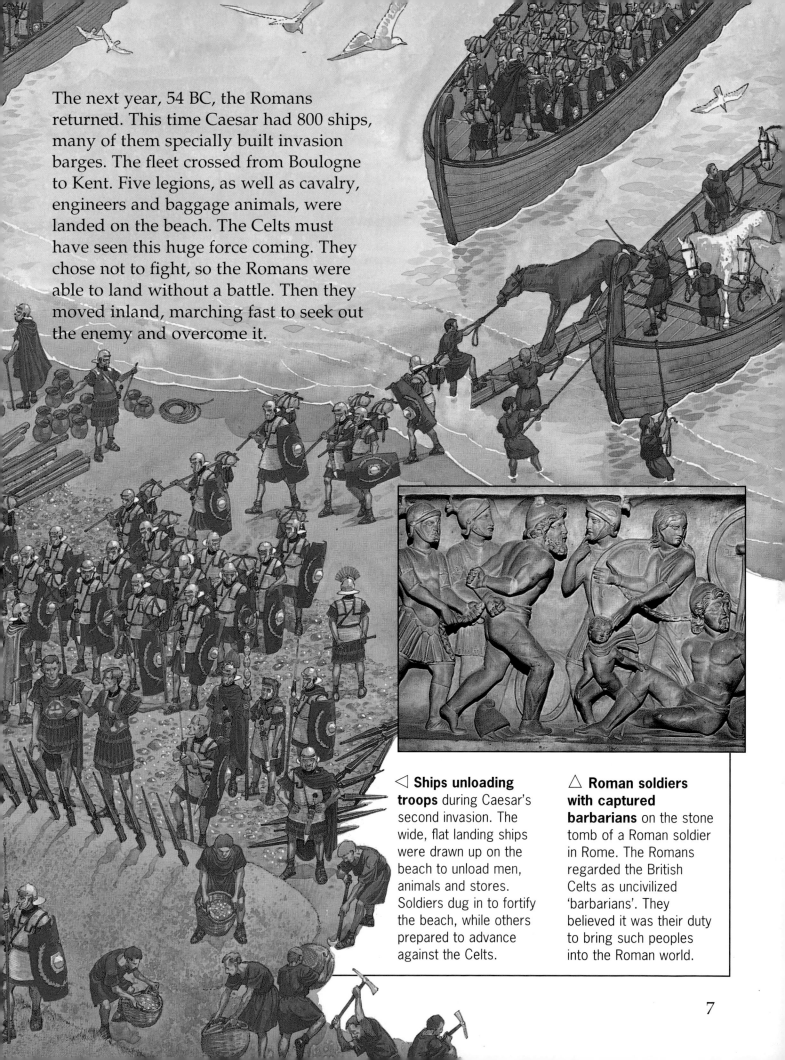

The next year, 54 BC, the Romans returned. This time Caesar had 800 ships, many of them specially built invasion barges. The fleet crossed from Boulogne to Kent. Five legions, as well as cavalry, engineers and baggage animals, were landed on the beach. The Celts must have seen this huge force coming. They chose not to fight, so the Romans were able to land without a battle. Then they moved inland, marching fast to seek out the enemy and overcome it.

◁ **Ships unloading troops** during Caesar's second invasion. The wide, flat landing ships were drawn up on the beach to unload men, animals and stores. Soldiers dug in to fortify the beach, while others prepared to advance against the Celts.

△ **Roman soldiers with captured barbarians** on the stone tomb of a Roman soldier in Rome. The Romans regarded the British Celts as uncivilized 'barbarians'. They believed it was their duty to bring such peoples into the Roman world.

VICTORY AND RETREAT

A captured Celt told Caesar that his people had "withdrawn and hidden themselves when they saw the numbers of our fleet". However, Caesar knew that a battle would be fought as soon as the Celtic chiefs could organize their followers into an army.

The retreating Celts took shelter inside a hill-fort at Bigbury near Canterbury. However, the Romans were used to attacking defended strongholds, and stormed the fort. The Celts fled. The Romans were about to pursue them, when Caesar learnt that storms and high tides in the Channel had damaged many of his ships. He had to hurry back to the coast, to make sure the ships were repaired and dragged up the beach well clear of the waves. This setback gave the Celts time to organize themselves.

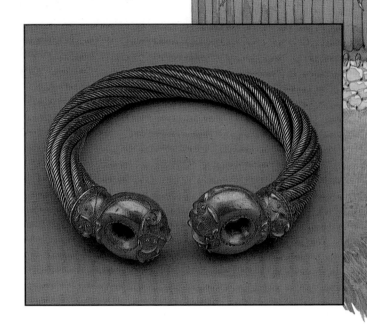

◁ **A Roman soldier's helmet** found in the River Thames in London. The Romans wore more armour than the Celts, some of whom fought practically naked.

△ **A Celtic gold torc** or neck ornament, found at Snettisham in Norfolk. Torcs were worn by important warriors. Coins found with this torc date it to 50 BC.

▷ **The attack on Bigbury fort.** The defenders blocked the gate with trees, but the soldiers of the 7th Legion advanced, protected by a wall of shields from the stones and spears hurled at them. They built a ramp, and then charged across the ditch and ramparts. Once inside the fort, the Romans used their short swords in fierce cut and thrust fighting – the kind of battle they usually won.

The Celts were now led by a chieftain named Cassivellaunus. They made surprise raids in horse-drawn chariots, which the Romans were unused to fighting. Still the legions marched on, until they crossed the River Thames. Now some Celts went over to the Romans' side. They guided them to the Celts' main camp; the Romans attacked and captured the Celts' stores and cattle. After this defeat, the Celts made peace. By the autumn, Caesar was back in Gaul.

The raid on Britain brought fame to Caesar, but little reward for Rome. However, the Romans had learnt much about the landscape, people and defences of Britain.

▷ **Romans fighting barbarians** (inset right), from a carving on Trajan's Column in Rome.

THE ROMANS RETURN

The Romans believed they had a mission to civilize the world. In the words of their poet Virgil, this was "to impose the ways of peace ... and to crush those proud men who will not submit". In AD 43 the Romans returned to Britain, this time to conquer.

▷ **After the battle of the Medway**, the victorious Romans raise their legion's standard above the fallen bodies of the enemy. The Celts fought bravely with their long swords, but lacked Roman discipline. Their leader was Caratacus, son of Cunobelinus. He escaped after the defeat.

In the 90 years following Caesar's raids, trade between southern Britain and the Roman empire flourished. Some Celtic chieftains were friendly to Rome and adopted Roman ways. Their coins have the Latin word *rex* (king) stamped on them. Grain, cattle, gold, iron, hides, slaves and dogs were traded across the Channel. Such riches tempted the Roman emperor, Claudius. He also had to keep his generals busy far from Rome, so they could not plot against him.

In AD 43, Claudius ordered an attack on Britain. The strongest chieftain in the island, Cunobelinus of the Catuvellauni, had died. The tribes of southern Britain were fighting among themselves. Claudius saw his opportunity. Rome would help friendly rulers, and get rid of troublemakers, in order to conquer Britain.

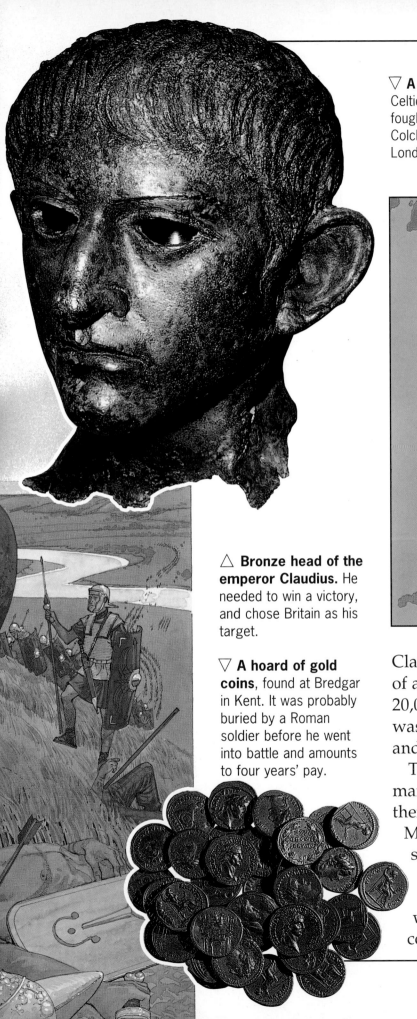

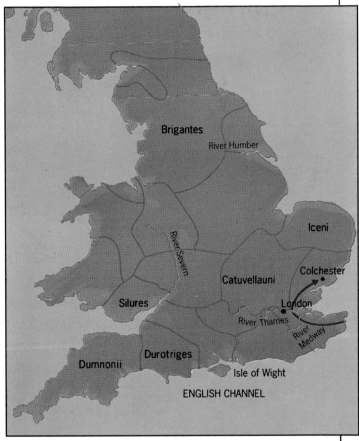

△ **A map of Britain.** It shows the lands of important Celtic tribes and, in red, where the Romans landed, fought the battle of the Medway, then marched on to Colchester. This was an important tribal capital. London was only a small settlement in those days.

△ **Bronze head of the emperor Claudius.** He needed to win a victory, and chose Britain as his target.

▽ **A hoard of gold coins**, found at Bredgar in Kent. It was probably buried by a Roman soldier before he went into battle and amounts to four years' pay.

Claudius' invasion army was made up of about 20,000 regular soldiers and 20,000 'auxiliaries'. The commander was Aulus Plautius, an experienced and skilled general.

The Romans landed in Kent, then marched inland. The Celts had gathered their army on the far bank of the River Medway. At night, auxiliary troops swam across and made a surprise attack on the chariots and horses of the Celts. Meanwhile, the legions waded the river at a shallow spot and completed the victory.

DIGGING IN

What we know about the Roman invasion of Britain comes from archaeological finds, and from histories written by the Romans. The Celts left no written accounts. Roman historians pointed to the main Celtic weakness. "They fight separately and separately are defeated," wrote Tacitus.

The Romans rapidly conquered south-east Britain. Split by tribal rivalries, the Celts were unable to defeat the invaders. Soon it was safe for Claudius to visit Britain, to parade in triumph through the tribal capital of Colchester. The defeated chieftains surrendered to the emperor. After two weeks Claudius returned to Rome, leaving his generals to conquer the rest of the island. The legions fanned out, marching north to Lincoln and the Midlands, and west as far as Exeter. Colchester became the capital of the new province of Roman Britain. However, some powerful local rulers were allowed to keep their lands. One was Cogidubnus, from whose lands in Hampshire and Sussex the Romans launched attacks on the west and the Isle of Wight.

△ **A gold coin of Cunobelinus.** The ear of wheat symbolized Britain's wealth.

▷ **Maiden Castle, in Dorset.** Even its impressive defences could not prevent its capture by the Romans around AD 43.

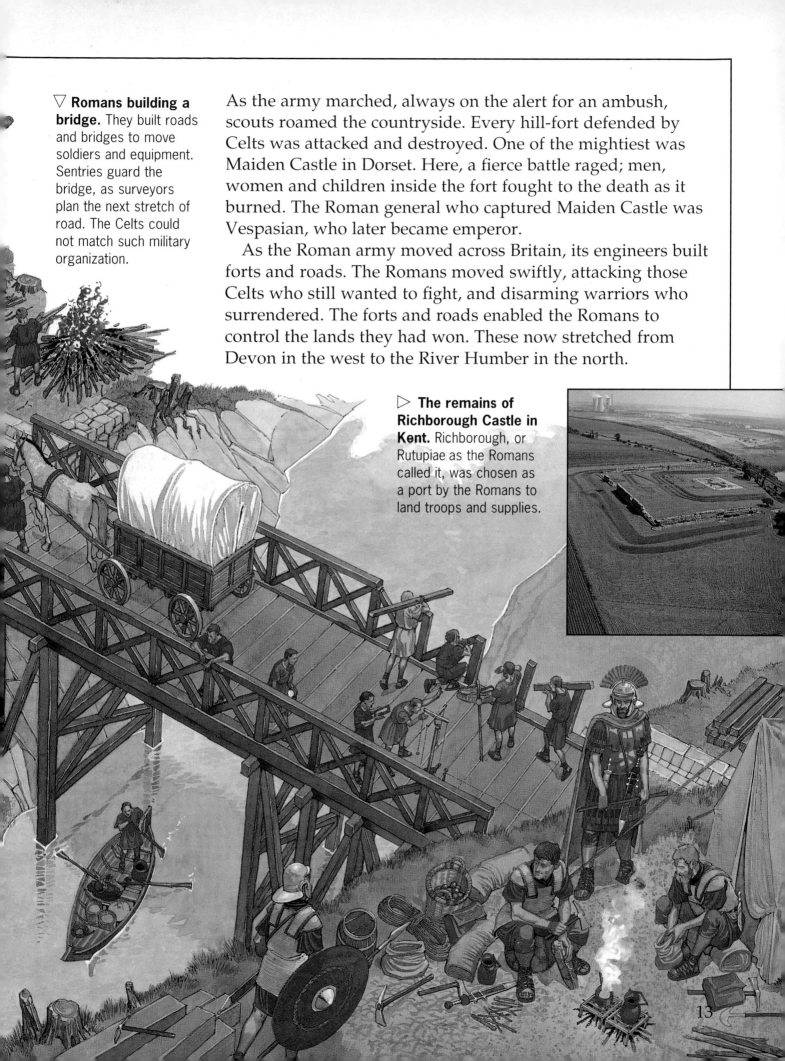

▽ **Romans building a bridge.** They built roads and bridges to move soldiers and equipment. Sentries guard the bridge, as surveyors plan the next stretch of road. The Celts could not match such military organization.

As the army marched, always on the alert for an ambush, scouts roamed the countryside. Every hill-fort defended by Celts was attacked and destroyed. One of the mightiest was Maiden Castle in Dorset. Here, a fierce battle raged; men, women and children inside the fort fought to the death as it burned. The Roman general who captured Maiden Castle was Vespasian, who later became emperor.

As the Roman army moved across Britain, its engineers built forts and roads. The Romans moved swiftly, attacking those Celts who still wanted to fight, and disarming warriors who surrendered. The forts and roads enabled the Romans to control the lands they had won. These now stretched from Devon in the west to the River Humber in the north.

▷ **The remains of Richborough Castle in Kent.** Richborough, or Rutupiae as the Romans called it, was chosen as a port by the Romans to land troops and supplies.

ROMAN SETTLERS

The Romans now held south-east Britain, with its mineral wealth (silver and iron) and good farmland. Beyond lay the mountains of Wales and northern Britain. In these remote regions, Celts waited and watched. The Romans were prepared to fight, but also to bargain, to hold on to what they had won.

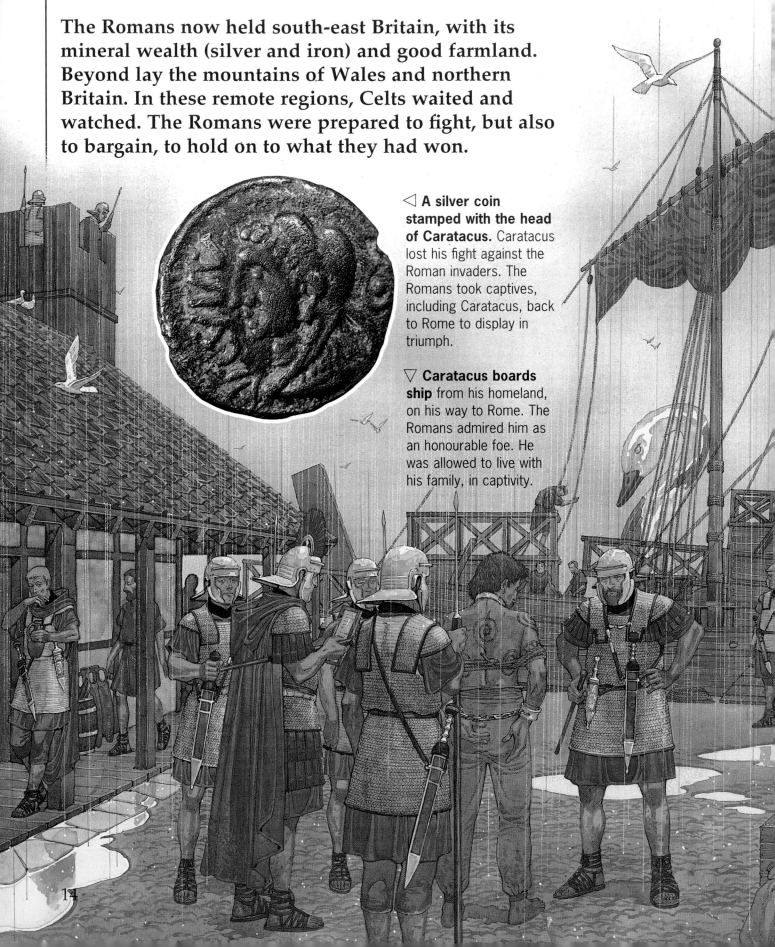

◁ **A silver coin stamped with the head of Caratacus.** Caratacus lost his fight against the Roman invaders. The Romans took captives, including Caratacus, back to Rome to display in triumph.

▽ **Caratacus boards ship** from his homeland, on his way to Rome. The Romans admired him as an honourable foe. He was allowed to live with his family, in captivity.

In the first 10 years after the invasion, the Roman soldiers worked hard. They built a network of forts and naval bases linked by roads. By about AD 50 the Romans had built a wooden bridge over the River Thames in London. This town was becoming an important centre for trade, especially shipping. The invaders also tried to make southern Britain 'Roman'. Colchester was made a 'colony' or settlement for old soldiers.

These soldier-settlers did two useful jobs. They kept local rebels in check, and they showed the Celts the advantages of the Roman way of life. But there were many complaints from Celtic nobles who had had their lands seized. Some became rebels and fled to join Caratacus, who was still fighting in the west.

Caratacus held out in the Welsh mountains until AD 51 when he was defeated at a battle in the Severn valley.

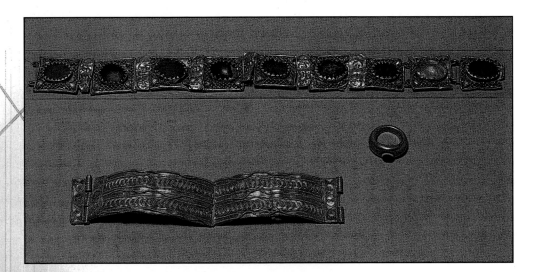

◁ **These jewelled bracelets** come from Rhayader in Powys, Wales, and date from AD 100-200. They may have been owned by Celtic nobles who had adopted Roman ways.

▽ **Hod Hill Fort (below left)**, in Dorset. It was captured by the Romans. They then built their own fort in one corner.

The battle proved to be a disaster for Caratacus. The Romans again overwhelmed the Celts, crossing the River Severn with ease and storming the enemy's hill-top fort.

Caratacus' wife and daughter were captured. Caratacus fled north, and gave himself up to the Brigantes. But their queen was an ally of the Romans. She handed him over to them as a sign of her loyalty. Caratacus was taken to Rome in chains. There his nobility impressed the emperor so much that he and his family were pardoned. The Romans were often ruthless, but by showing Caratacus mercy they hoped to achieve peace.

MAKING ENEMIES

Many Celts resented the Romans. The Greek historian Dio Cassius described Boudicca urging the Iceni: "Do not fear the Romans... they are hares and foxes trying to rule over dogs and wolves."

The Iceni of East Anglia were a strong and independent people. Since they controlled important sea routes from northern Europe into eastern Britain, the Romans were keen to win their support. At first, the Iceni seemed willing. However, in AD 47 the Romans tried to limit their freedom by taking away their weapons. The Iceni rose in defiance. It was a foretaste of a more serious challenge to Rome.

▷ **Colchester Castle.** The central stronghold of the existing castle was built by Normans in about 1080 on the site of, and using stonework from, the Roman Temple of Claudius. In the soil beneath the modern city itself, archaeologists have found a layer of soot and ash – evidence of the burning of the Roman city.

△ **Tombstone of a Roman soldier.** The stone may have been pushed over by the rebels, which by chance protected the carving.

In AD 54 Claudius died, and his stepson Nero became emperor. About four years later, he appointed a new governor of Britain. This was Suetonius Paulinus, an expert in mountain warfare. In AD 60 Paulinus led an army into the mountains of north Wales. The Celts had a stronghold on the island of Anglesey, where refugees and Druids had gathered. The Romans attacked, defying the priests' curses, and a bloody massacre followed. They smashed the altars on which slaves and captives had been sacrificed.

One bloody fight was soon followed by another. This time the Romans faced a mass uprising. It began in Colchester, the meeting place of the council that governed Roman Britain. The city had been peaceful. Now it was in flames.

◁ **The Celts attack the temple in Colchester.**
The new stone temple had been put up to honour Claudius and was hated as a symbol of Roman power. The city had few defences and its wooden houses were quickly ablaze. There was much slaughter. A small group of Roman soldiers defended the temple until they too were killed.

▽ **Iceni coins**, found in Cambridgeshire. They were probably hidden for safekeeping during the revolt.

The Romans had treated the people of Colchester badly. Officials had seized private land and houses, as gifts for retired soldiers. The Celts felt that they were being treated like slaves. Now the Iceni of Norfolk rose again, joining forces with their southern neighbours, the Trinovantes. They accused the Romans of plundering their lands, and ill-treating the Iceni queen Boudicca and her daughters.

The Roman legions were far away in the Midlands and Wales. Led by Boudicca, the rebels swept down on Colchester. After a short siege, they stormed the city. Romans, and Celts who had worked for the Romans, fled in panic. Those who did not escape were slaughtered. The rebels feasted to celebrate victory, and then moved east towards London.

THE GREAT REVOLT

"The Britons took no prisoners ... it was as if they feared that retribution [punishment] might catch up with them," wrote the Roman historian Tacitus. As the Roman army struggled to regroup, the great revolt led by Boudicca threatened Rome's hold on Britain. London fell, amid great bloodshed.

After Colchester, the Celts soon attacked St Albans. This city had been the stronghold of the Catuvellauni. Now it too had bright new Roman buildings. They were looted and burned. The Celtic army moved on.

A small Roman force tried to check the rebels east of London, but was quickly cut to pieces. Only the cavalry escaped. Governor Suetonius Paulinus rushed to London ahead of his legions. He decided he could not defend the city, and withdrew. Londoners who were able to, fled with the troops. The rest stayed.

They found no mercy from the rebels: Romans and Celts alike were killed. The rebels then spread out in roving bands, seeking more Roman settlements to loot. The Roman histories tell of dreadful massacres and tortures. Some 70,000 "Roman citizens and friends of Rome" were slain by Boudicca's forces.

Three Roman cities lay in ruins. The Roman army, regrouping in the Midlands, was outnumbered. Boudicca was now at the head of a horde of at least 120,000 warriors – a force probably ten times that of the Romans.

▷ **Before the battle in the Midlands.** The rebels had many chariots and wagons, but most of their warriors fought on foot. The Romans lined up on the hill-top. At the start of the battle, the rebels charged up the slope, but were halted by a hail of javelins. Then the Roman infantry advanced, flanked by archers and cavalry. The rebels were driven back and became entangled with baggage wagons and horses.

▷ **Fire damage caused by the attack on London** can still be seen in soil layers. The black surface is the charred remains of burnt timber buildings.

▷ **Evidence of the havoc in London.** These are the remains of buildings destroyed when Boudicca's army swept into the city. The traces of this violent destruction now lie buried beneath the busy streets and offices of the modern City of London.

A decisive battle now took place. The Romans chose their battleground with care. They drew up their troops in three close-ranked divisions; a wood protected their backs. The rebels appeared in a swarming mass, shouting battle-cries. Watched by their families from carts drawn up behind, and sure of victory, they charged. As so often before, Roman discipline triumphed. The battle ended with the Celts in flight. Soon afterwards, Boudicca was dead; she probably took poison to avoid capture.

◁ **This skull may be from a Roman victim** of Boudicca's revolt in AD 60. It was found in the Walbrook, a small river in London.

19

REVENGE AND RECOVERY

After Boudicca's death, the rebels were leaderless. Now the Romans took their revenge, both on tribes that had joined the revolt, and those which had not. This might have led to more uprisings. But then the Romans changed their policy, and the Celts accepted peace. It was a chance to rebuild.

The Romans were determined to crush all resistance. Fresh troops came from Germany, and Roman soldiers burnt villages and fields. Such a cruel policy only made matters worse. During the revolt, no crops had been planted and now many Celts faced starvation. Worse still, from the Romans' point of view, they were unable to pay their taxes.

The Romans were usually very practical. Now a tax official sent an urgent message to Rome, informing Nero that Britain was being mismanaged.

▷ **The tombstone of a Roman cavalryman**, found at Gloucester. He came from Thrace in the Balkans. Like many of his comrades, he fought and died a long way from home.

▷ **Remains of a Roman bridge and quay in London.**
Wooden beams stick out from part of the wall of a possible bridge support base (left), the rest of which is covered by modern concrete (right). The remains were recently discovered on the north bank of the River Thames. The bridge is believed to date from the time of the revolt of AD 60.

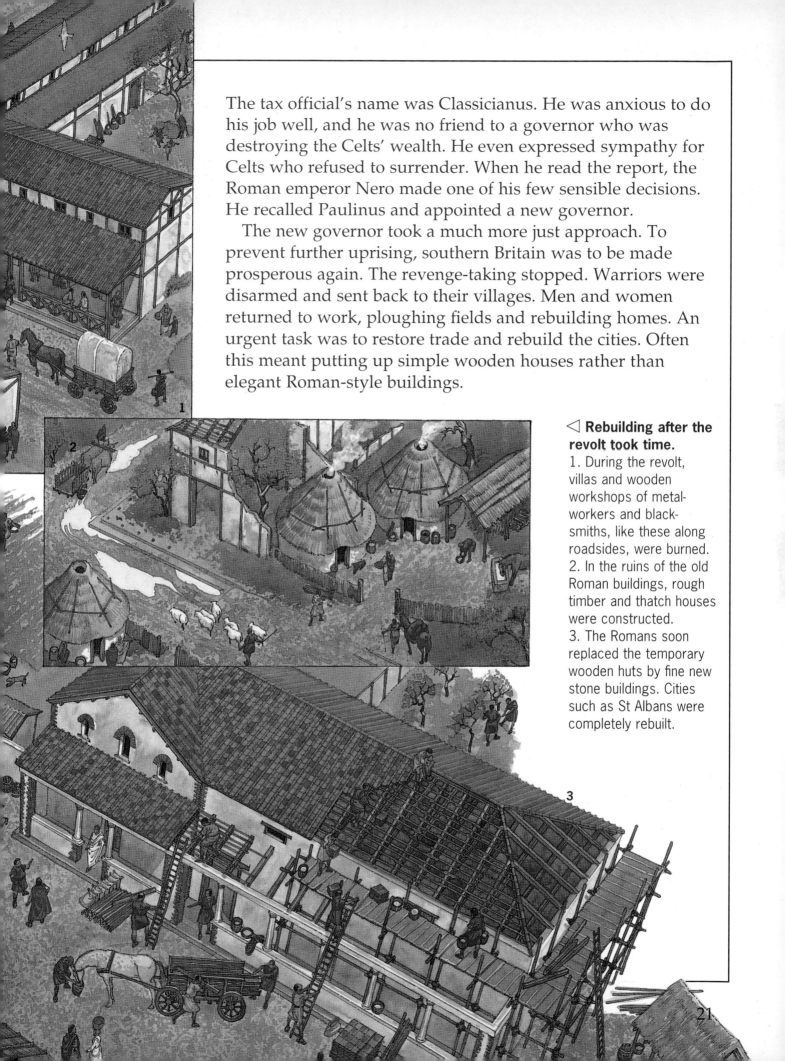

The tax official's name was Classicianus. He was anxious to do his job well, and he was no friend to a governor who was destroying the Celts' wealth. He even expressed sympathy for Celts who refused to surrender. When he read the report, the Roman emperor Nero made one of his few sensible decisions. He recalled Paulinus and appointed a new governor.

The new governor took a much more just approach. To prevent further uprising, southern Britain was to be made prosperous again. The revenge-taking stopped. Warriors were disarmed and sent back to their villages. Men and women returned to work, ploughing fields and rebuilding homes. An urgent task was to restore trade and rebuild the cities. Often this meant putting up simple wooden houses rather than elegant Roman-style buildings.

◁ **Rebuilding after the revolt took time.**
1. During the revolt, villas and wooden workshops of metal-workers and black-smiths, like these along roadsides, were burned.
2. In the ruins of the old Roman buildings, rough timber and thatch houses were constructed.
3. The Romans soon replaced the temporary wooden huts by fine new stone buildings. Cities such as St Albans were completely rebuilt.

BUILDING ROMAN BRITAIN

In the 20 years after the invasion of AD 43, the Romans had conquered southern Britain. Now they could turn their attention to the north of the island. They never fully controlled northern Britain. But under Roman rule, southern Britain enjoyed 400 years of peace and prosperity.

There was much rebuilding to be done. Many farms and villas, built since the invasion, lay in ruins. Fields were unploughed and weed-choked.

The Romans tried to win the support of the Celtic nobles. They restored their wealth, so that they could enjoy the benefits of Roman rule. New Roman-style villas and towns were built to replace those destroyed in the revolt. To guard against future rebellion, the Roman army built more roads, and larger fortresses like those at Gloucester, Chester and York. The legions stayed prepared for war. Even friendly tribes like the northern Brigantes swiftly became enemies under a new leader.

Southern Britain was still a frontier province. But the well-planned invasion had succeeded in making it yet another part of the Roman Empire.

▽ **Part of the Roman villa** at Lullingstone in Kent. Tiled steps lead to the cellar, where there were several rooms. At the bottom of the steps, on the right was a shrine set into the wall.

▷ **Bronze head of Hadrian**, who in AD 122 ordered a wall to be built in north Britain to mark the frontier of Roman rule.

▷ **The Roman town of Caerwent in Wales** was built around AD 100 on the site of a Celtic town. This picture shows the remains of houses with shops fronting on to the street. Some of the houses had many rooms and were as elegant as those built in Rome.

GLOSSARY

alliance an agreement, between **allies** or friendly groups, to work or fight together.

auxiliary soldier in the Roman army who was not a Roman citizen, but a foreigner.

cavalry soldiers on horseback.

Celts people living in Britain and western Europe at the time of the Roman conquest.

citizen a man who was allowed to vote in elections.

Druids Celtic priests who were also lawmakers and judges. Druidism involved worship of many gods.

emperor supreme ruler of Rome.

fleet group of warships.

frontier boundary between one area and another.

Gaul Roman province (it covered what is now France, Belgium and the Rhine region of Germany). Its people were known as Gauls.

governor Roman official in charge of a province.

hill-fort Celtic fort, usually with ditches, earth banks and fences on high ground.

hypocaust central heating system in houses, using underfloor hot air.

infantry soldiers on foot.

javelin throwing spear.

Latin language of the Romans.

legion Roman military unit, with from 4,000 to 6,000 soldiers (known as legionaries).

province an area within the Roman empire, such as Gaul.

revolt uprising by rebels against the rulers of a country.

standard legion's ceremonial pole, carried into battle.

taxes money collected by the government from the people to pay for new roads and buildings, or to equip the army.

villa a farm with a house and outbuildings, or a large country house.

▷ **This map** shows the main roads and towns of Roman Britain. (Town names then were in Latin – London, for example, was called Londinium.) The roads fanned out from the south-east, where the Romans first landed. Roads from London included Watling Street, which went to the fortress-towns of Wroxeter and Chester. The Fosse Way marked the frontier from Exeter in the west to Lincoln and the River Humber in the east. Other roads linked important cities, such as Colchester and St Albans, and key ports, such as Dover.

THE SHETLANDS

—— Proven routes
--- Suspected routes

23

INDEX